FORGIVENESS

Also by Marjorie J. Thompson
from Westminster John Knox Press

Soul Feast: An Invitation to the Christian Spiritual Life

FORGIVENESS

A Lenten Study

MARJORIE J. THOMPSON

WESTMINSTER
JOHN KNOX PRESS
LOUISVILLE • KENTUCKY

Portions of this book were previously published as a downloadable study titled "Learning Forgiveness: A Lenten Study," The Thoughtful Christian, January 13, 2010, www.TheThoughtfulChristian.com.

First edition
Published by Westminster John Knox Press
Louisville, Kentucky

14 15 16 17 18 19 20 21 22 23—10 9 8 7 6 5 4 3 2 1

Book design by Erika Lundbom
Cover design by Dilu Nicholas

Library of Congress Cataloging-in-Publication Data
Thompson, Marjorie J., 1953-
Forgiveness : a Lenten study / Marjorie J. Thompson. — First edition.
pages cm
Includes bibliographical references.
ISBN 978-0-664-25972-3 (alk. paper)
1. Forgiveness—Religious aspects—Christianity—Study and teaching.
2. Lent--Meditations. I. Title.
BV4647.F55T47 2014
234'.5—dc23

2013041187

♾The paper used in this publication meets the minimum requirements of the American National Standard for Information Sciences—Permanence of Paper for Printed Library Materials, ANSI Z39.48-1992.

Most Westminster John Knox Press books are available at special quantity discounts when purchased in bulk by corporations, organizations, and special-interest groups. For more information, please e-mail SpecialSales@wjkbooks.com.

CONTENTS

INTRODUCTION

THERE IS "NO FUTURE WITHOUT FORGIVENESS," ARCHBISHOP Desmond Tutu argues compellingly in his book by that title. Raised in a culture that values a rich sense of community, Tutu brings our deep human yearning for communal harmony to bear on the aftermath of Black oppression under the systemic injustices of Apartheid in South Africa. At the least, we can say that without forgiveness there is no future worthy of human life and community as God surely intended them to be in the originating vision of Creation. Moreover, we now have a better sense than we did half a century ago that "no future" in the human community invariably implicates the future of the planet and all its life forms. We are inextricably connected. If we cannot find our way to healthy human communities, we will inevitably damage the earth and likely perish together.

There is also no Christianity without forgiveness. It is impossible to conceive of any expression of Christian discipleship that ignores or excludes a virtue so central to the good news. The entire message of Jesus' life, death, and resurrection would be lost without it. Forgiveness is the healing stream flowing out from the crucified Christ over a world that does not know how desperately it needs the healing. Yet divine forgiveness—what Christ on the cross represents—is precisely what makes a realistic future possible within a human community still largely wading around in the muck of emotional and spiritual immaturity.

If we imagine humanity as evolving toward higher levels of consciousness, we could say that perhaps on balance we have entered early adolescence. In most parts of the world, the ethic of retaliation and revenge is hugely popular, supported even by holy writ. We are captive to the ego-centered perceptions and reactions of our "reptilian brain," the brain stem governing our instincts for survival and security. Inside this primitive cognitive center—alive and well in all of us—empathy with others does not exist. When we are deeply fearful or traumatized, we revert unconsciously to our instinctual brain. Consequently, the more conflict we experience, the more likely we are to participate in and create further conflict. Violence begets violence, trauma thrusts us away from the higher cognitive functions that allow a more civil society to be nurtured and sustained.

A particularly significant word here is "unconscious." When Jesus is crucified, he offers God a rationale for divine forgiveness: "They don't know what they are doing." This could still be said of most people on the planet today. We have little idea of what we are actually doing. We judge others and ourselves based on outward words and actions, but we don't comprehend the deeper reaches of mind and heart from which they arise. So much of what we see, do, and say is rooted in unconscious wounds and unmet needs. Our insecurity and anxiety shape how we perceive others—as rivals or allies, objects of envy or objects to be despised, enemies out to get us or people "like us"—and therefore how we react to them in speech and behavior.

Unconscious ego manipulations, at both personal and corporate levels, wreak enormous damage in human relationships. But if these operations are largely unconscious, we need to stop judging our egos so harshly! The defenses and ploys of the ego have been nurtured from infancy to defend our security and bolster our sense of control in a world full of pain, incomprehension, and chaos. The program we need to undertake, in order to move a skittish ego out of the driver's seat of our lives, is to understand its felt needs and exercise compassion for its anxieties and compulsions. As we come to recognize the way ego functions, we can gradually let go of its demands, releasing the immature sense of self and welcoming our more mature identity. That more mature identity finds its full expression in Christ, "the image of the invisible God" (Col. 1:15). We, too, are made in the divine image, but it is deeply hidden under the creaky structures of security and control we have tried to fashion for ourselves.

God's forgiveness offers us a way to move forward: to challenge the assumed supremacy of our small ego-kingdoms; to discover our common humanity with others of all backgrounds; to wake up to the deeper reality of our identity in Christ. In him, we can grow up into the full maturity of mind, heart, and spirit that is our true human inheritance. I hope the pages that follow will give us a chance to explore this terrain with others who yearn for a better way. Shall we enter this remarkable adventure together?

Chapter 1

BEGINNINGS

A Kinship Appeal

Luke 15:11–32

THE CHRISTIAN FAITH IS INDELIBLY MARKED BY THE
invitation to receive, and the imperative to offer, forgiveness. Forgiveness is the fountain from which new
life flows in a wounded, strife-weary world. It can be
reasonably argued that the idea of forgiveness is more
central and distinctive to Christianity than to any other
religion, although most great faith traditions give at
least some weight to it. Jesus' forgiveness from the cross
of those who crucified him is a profound embodiment
of what he taught and reveals this centrality.

Whether the followers of Jesus actually practice
forgiveness more than persons of other faiths can be
questioned. Perhaps this is, in part, because Christians
differ widely in their interpretations of how forgiveness
should be practiced.

- Some urge forgiveness as a Christian duty under all circumstances, while others argue that certain conditions must be met before forgiveness can be meaningful or effective.
- Some see forgiveness as a matter between particular individuals, and some regard it as meaningful only in the context of larger human communities.
- Some believe forgiving is the surest route to healing for the injured, while others hold that therapy cannot be the essence of Christian forgiveness.

How do we sort through such competing claims and interpretations? What is the core of this powerful gift we are called to participate in? And how do we get past some of our emotional barriers to real forgiveness? These are the kinds of the questions we will explore together in this study of a theme that is particularly well suited to the season of Lent but fit for any season of our lives.

The aim of this study is threefold: (1) to listen to a variety of voices, including our own; (2) to discern some complexities of the subject and then to claim our own biblically and theologically informed stance; and, perhaps most importantly, (3) to begin a few practices that will help us develop a mind and heart oriented toward forgiveness.

WHO NEEDS FORGIVENESS?

Let's start with a familiar parable—that of the Prodigal Son (Luke 15). We tend to assume that only one of the three main characters of this story needs forgiveness. It is, after all, the younger son who demands his portion of his father's inheritance before even a hint of his father's demise. In traditional Near Eastern culture, this would have been inexcusable behavior in its own right. He then blunders forward into ruin, squandering his entire fortune in "high living" and finding himself broke in the face of unexpected famine. It is hard to sympathize with a young man so self-absorbed and foolish. The last straw to Jewish ears would have been his complete self-degradation by hiring himself out to a pig farmer. Not only has this son dishonored his father and led a morally reprehensible life, but he has defiled himself by association with unclean animals.

Certainly this young man needs to turn himself around and seek forgiveness. His sins are abundantly clear. Sure enough, once he realizes his predicament and remembers what his father's household is like, he undergoes an inward repentance. His mental speech to his father reveals first an admission of offense ("I have sinned against heaven and before you") and then a turn to shame and humility ("I am no longer worthy to be called your son; treat me like one of your hired hands"). Everything is in order so far. The younger son is in need of forgiveness and has taken steps that could make his father's forgiveness possible.

But this story is not so simple. The father in this tale does not act like a typical Middle Eastern patriarch, gravely standing on his authority, testing the authenticity of his younger son's intentions, and slowly relenting on his own legitimate grievances. This father acts like a Jewish mama incurably attached to a youngest child.

After rushing forward to embrace his filthy boy, not even waiting for him to finish his repentance speech, he orders up a big party to celebrate the return of this extravagant waster of wealth. Is the father acting responsibly? Is his behavior excusable? Does he need to be forgiven for allowing his emotions to rule the day, for acting without dignity or justice?

Apparently the older brother thinks so. He is appalled by what he sees his father doing upon his younger brother's return. The elder son feels the sting of injustice keenly. He has been dutiful, respectful, and responsible all his life. He has done everything according to law and custom, yet his father has never thrown a party to celebrate his right living. What he surely sees is an obvious breach of equity in his father's treatment of his two sons. His father, it seems, just takes his older son for granted and shows clear favoritism toward the younger son.

The elder brother suffers self-righteous indignation. He feels aggrieved about how his father welcomes back the younger son, without conditions or any apparent concern for justice. We can imagine how the elder son's resentment of his brother arose when the younger made a premature claim on his share of the family inheritance. This resentment surely grew deeper over the period of time his brother was absent. Reports of reckless, wasteful, and immoral behavior must have come back through the grapevine, shaming and dishonoring the family's reputation. No doubt the older brother's heart had long since closed toward his younger brother. He suffered from a hard heart, a sclerosis of love. Did he also need his father's forgiveness?

Did these two brothers need to forgive each other as well?

Perhaps we can now begin to see the complexity of this simple parable. Jesus seems to want us to grapple with various forms of alienation from each other and from God. Perhaps he hopes we will learn to see ourselves in this story in more than one way.

AN INDIVIDUAL OR COMMUNAL AFFAIR?

Some would say forgiveness is primarily an individual matter, that individuals are responsible for their own bad decisions or attitudes and no one else is to blame. Certainly with respect to God, each soul must speak from its own conscience to its life choices before the Creator. The position promoting individual accountability for sin is easy to grasp and widely held.

Others argue that forgiveness is primarily about life in a community of persons rather than about isolated individuals. Human minds, hearts, and lives are shaped by communities and in turn impact communities. We arrive at ideas, decisions, and actions in the context of relationships. Is it then fair to attribute a person's poor choices entirely to that one individual? Are not others at least partly implicated? A failed marriage or friendship is rarely the entire fault of one partner. This position on forgiveness is less evident and messier to sort out. It involves asking what systemic failures within families, schools, churches, businesses, or governing structures may contribute to personal moral and ethical failures. It invites us to consider whether we are unwitting enablers or even coconspirators with the fallen among us.

The story of the Prodigal Son suggests that matters of forgiveness are not always as clear as they first appear. In this case, both brothers need their father's forgiveness for different offenses. To Jesus' Jewish audience, the younger brother would be the obvious case, and no doubt Jesus painted his character to make it as obvious as possible. But Jesus is also speaking to the good, upright Pharisees of his time (and ours) in the figure of the older brother. The subtler message of this story, for those with ears to hear, is that our self-righteous judgment against obvious sinners places us in the same boat with them before God. Indeed, our need of forgiveness may be greater because we do not see it and can therefore hide under the illusion that we are without sin while pointing the finger at others. In psychological terms, this is called projection. We do not see the darkness within us, so we conveniently project it onto those we can easily label as wrongdoers.

Jesus had a lot to say about this form of sin. Many of his warnings to the serious religious folk of his day pointed to the trap of self-righteous judgment. His parable of the Pharisee and the Tax Collector (Luke 18:9–14) is told "to some who trusted in themselves that they were righteous and regarded others with contempt" (v. 9). Another example is this sharp question in the Sermon on the Mount, set in the context of warning against judging others: "Why do you see the speck in your neighbor's eye but do not notice the log in your own eye?" (Matt. 7:3).

Forgiveness in a family is generally a complex affair rooted in years of messy personal dynamics. In the parable of the Prodigal Son, we might well imagine strains between the two brothers long before the younger decided to depart, strains that possibly contributed to his desire to leave. We might wonder what the father's relationship with each son had been like, or at least how each son perceived his father in relation to himself and his brother. We wonder because we have grown up in families and have our own experiences with parents and siblings that evoke feelings of empathy with, or resistance to, these characters.

The matter here is whether human forgiveness is about broader relationships than merely the spiritual and psychological needs of individuals. While the needs of individuals are always deeply relevant, the larger picture is one of human beings thrown together in multiple relationships that intersect in a complex web of love, friendship, miscommunication, self-interest, hurt, healing, and reconciliation.

Scholar Gregory Jones argues that if we start our ideas about forgiveness with the isolated individual, we'll get it wrong. The starting point is God—a community of persons within a profound and mysterious unity we call the Holy Trinity. Forgiveness is an outpouring of love from the inner life of the Trinity and can only be fully understood when experienced as a transforming power in the life of a human community that mirrors God's being.

A DEEPER KINSHIP STORY

Ella Cara Deloria tells a story of life among the Dakota Sioux Indians that illustrates the less obvious, communal dynamics of forgiveness. A young man in the tribe had been murdered, and his enraged relatives were gathered to plan revenge. The eldest male in the clan listened to them talk out their aggrieved feelings and vindictive intentions, repeating to them what he heard them say. He then smoked quietly and calmly for a while. Finally, he spoke again to say that there was a better way—a harder but better way that they would take. He told them to go home, look over their possessions, and bring back the one thing they prized most.

> The gifts you bring shall go to the murderer, for a token of our sincerity and our purpose. Though he has hurt us, we shall make him . . . [a relative], in place of the one who is not here. Was the dead your brother? Then this man shall be your brother. . . . As for me, the dead was my nephew. Therefore, his slayer shall be my nephew. And from now on he shall be one of us. We shall regard him as though he were our dead kinsman returned to us.[1]

This "harder way" demanded of each person in the clan a powerful inner struggle to master pride, anger, and desire for revenge. But they accepted the challenge, because they could see that it was deeply right. They realized that a violent response would only fuel fires of hate over time but that the difficult task of taking this man into their family on a daily basis had the potential to heal them all. At the appointed time, the murderer was brought into the council tepee and given the peace pipe with these words:

> Smoke, with these your new kinsmen seated here. For they have chosen to take you to themselves in place of

one who is not here. . . . It is their desire that hence-
forth you shall go in and out among them without
fear. By these presents which they have brought here
for you, they would have you know that whatever
love and compassion they had for him is now yours,
forever.[2]

Deeply moved, the slayer began to weep. The narrator
then remarks that this man will surely prove himself
the best possible kinsman, given the high price of his
redemption.

This incident is a story of forgiveness, although the
Sioux elder never used that term. The characters spoke
in terms of kinship. Their act of reconciliation was pre-
sented as a way to make their extended family whole
once more, filling the empty place of the departed with
the very one responsible for his death. It was a corporate act of forgiveness that was simultaneously a profound act of communal self-healing and peacemaking.
The effect was to reknit the badly torn fabric of their
community.

By hearing and acting on their elder's wisdom, the
Sioux tribe was able to grasp the truth of their humanity in common with a violent offender. The act of
selecting and bringing a prized possession from each
home was a way of symbolizing the giving of themselves to the offender. It required them to acknowledge
and act on their deeper sense of human identification
with each other.

In taking the slayer into their hearts in place of the
relative he killed, this extended family grasped the need
for their whole community to heal a heart-wrenching
wound. They understood their common humanity

with the offender as a fundamental resource for reconciliation. Such a perspective is more often found among indigenous peoples than among those shaped by the rationalism and individualism of Western culture. Indeed, such a perspective stands as a profound challenge to our ordinary way of thinking. Yet perhaps our Christian faith offers us a way to connect the Sioux kinship appeal with Jesus' life and teaching.

FORGIVENESS, COMMUNION, AND RENEWAL

As human beings, we are all created in the same image and likeness—God's. There is a deep well of life from which we come and to which we return. According to Quaker writer Douglas Steere, our souls "are interconnected in God, as though the many wicks of our lamps draw their oil from the same full cruse in which they are all immersed."[3] God made us for communion with our Creator, with each other, and with the whole natural order. The Genesis story of Eden paints a picture of such harmonious relationships, and the Hebrew concept of *shalom*—peaceful and holistic well-being—expresses it well.

If we are spiritually united by virtue of our creation, however, we are sorrowfully united as well in our fall from the grace of such unity. All of us are alienated in various degrees from God, one another, the created order, and our true selves. Yet while our broken relationships cause terrible harm and division in this world, the spiritual truth of our human commonality remains intact. God's love unites us by invisible bonds.

It is a spiritual reality we know and claim in Christ, even though our churches are often sad case studies in human conflict.

The communion we were made for is the life Christ came to renew. We participate in this renewal each time we celebrate Holy Communion. Perhaps it should not surprise us that the Native American peace-pipe ritual bears some parallel to this Christian sacrament. Each man smoking the common pipe is reminded of his own center, which is understood at the same time to be the center of each person and of the whole universe. Do we not also understand that Christ dwells deep down— if unrecognized—in every person? ("Just as you did it to one of the least of these . . . , you did it to me" [Matt. 25:40]). And that Christ dwells at the core of the cosmos? ("All things have been created through him and for him. . . . And in him all things hold together" [Col. 1:16–17]). He is our unity who has reconciled us all to God. In the restoration of communion with God and each other, Christ brings us renewed life. At the heart of this new life lies the gift of divine forgiveness. Yet in order to receive such mercy, we must first see how much we need it.

Chapter 2

SELF-EXAMINATION

Prelude to Forgiveness

Psalms 51 and 139

THE NEED FOR SELF-EXAMINATION

Along the path of his "triumphal entry" into Jerusalem from the Mount of Olives, as he is riding a young colt and receiving the acclaim of the crowd, Jesus catches sight of the city and laments over it: "If you, even you, had only recognized on this day the things that make for peace!" (Luke 19:42). Forgiving others is one of the key things that make for peace, as Jesus will reveal and embody in his own approaching passion; the renewal of harmonious, spiritually healthy relationships with God and others is the whole purpose of his incarnation. How do we open ourselves to the magnitude of this gift?

One of the greatest impediments to recognizing what makes for peace is our reluctance to look closely at our own hearts—what we are actually feeling, imagining, assuming, or pondering. Engaged in ordinary routines, we sometimes move through life like sleepwalkers, not fully conscious of what we experience. It takes a certain level of awareness to name what we are thinking or feeling at any given time. But even when circumstances or relationships are striking enough to sharpen our awareness, all sorts of inner filters—preconceptions, unspoken fears, illusions—can distort an accurate reading of our thoughts and feelings. Consequently, we often react to things without noticing the real motives behind our actions.

If we cannot see how our minds and hearts actually operate and how they resist the things that make for health and peace, we will not be able to admit what alienates us from God, others, or ourselves. What we cannot acknowledge we cannot confess, and what we cannot confess we cannot present for forgiveness and healing.

Awareness, acknowledgment, and confession are the foundation for seeking and receiving forgiveness. That is why self-examination is one of the chief spiritual exercises of the Christian life, especially fitting for Lenten practice. Self-examination is the spiritual art of paying close attention to the dynamics of our hearts and minds. It requires of us nondefensive honesty and humility before God.

Two fundamental truths undergird the practice of self-examination.[1] First, God loves us without conditions.

We can neither earn nor deserve God's love; it is a gift, waiting to be received by faith and trust. Certainly we can disappoint and distance ourselves from God, but we cannot fall below or outside the web of divine love pervading the whole cosmos. Until we grasp this truth at the emotional core of our being, we will not find sufficient courage to engage in honest and healthy self-reflection. Either we will feel compelled to stretch the truth in order to preserve some shreds of pride, rationalizing our words and acts before One whose love we do not fully trust, or we will collapse into unhealthy self-recrimination, whipping and cursing ourselves in the punishments of self-hatred. Neither of these reactions will help us find healing and wholeness in Christ. God's absolutely unconditional love gives us solid ground on which to stand with the security we need for unflinching honesty.

Second, we are, each and all of us, fallen human beings. There are no exceptions to the fact that we are sinners, just as there are no exceptions to God's overwhelming love for each of us. Sin is a deeply rooted disorientation in which we tend to see all things primarily in relation to ourselves rather than in relation to God. Everything revolves around the central sun of our little egos. Whether we tend toward the illusion of grandiosity or the illusion of worthlessness, the essence of sin is self-absorption. In its ten thousand expressions, bold and subtle, it remains a persistent framework of the human condition.

Without the first truth, we could not find comfort in seeking God's help or summon strength with that help to see ourselves clearly. Without the second truth, there would be no need for confession or forgiveness.

Two particular psalms can effectively tutor us in self-examination, helping us more truthfully to observe our spiritual condition. The first is Psalm 51, that classic psalm of penitence used in corporate prayer on Ash Wednesday to mark the beginning of Lent. The second is Psalm 139, one of the most beloved of all psalms for its wondering gaze into the mystery of God's identity and our own. These two psalms reveal two sides of self-examination: examination of conscience and examination of consciousness.

PSALM 51 AND EXAMINATION OF CONSCIENCE

Psalm 51 is a cry from the depths of the soul for God's mercy and cleansing. It expresses great certainty about our human need for what only God can provide: the blotting out of transgression, the cleansing of sin, the purging of iniquity, the re-creation of a pure heart, the giving of wisdom, and the restoration of a right and willing spirit. Here is a prayer that recognizes guilt from the moment of birth and acknowledges that all sin is first and foremost directed against God. It is a penitential psalm of confession and plea for pardon.

Not surprisingly, Psalm 51 has been interpreted through the millennia as King David's cry for divine mercy after his wretched episode with Bathsheba (see 2 Sam. 11). How easy it is for us to forget the full measure of David's sin. First, he indulged in adultery with Bathsheba while her husband, Uriah, was off fighting the king's battles. Then, in an attempt to disguise Bathsheba's resulting pregnancy, David tried twice to manipulate Uriah into breaking military conduct in order to sleep with his wife. When these efforts to cover his tracks failed, David resorted to a successful plot with his army commander to get Uriah killed in battle. The whole sorry tale is worthy of an opera. But with our human penchant for drama, we easily recognize and understand the dynamics of David's story. One offense often draws us into further ill-conceived acts to cover the first. We soon find ourselves on a trail of deceit and manipulation, trying desperately to keep the original offense secret and often implicating others in our sordid ploys.

Psalm 51 is a vivid expression of examination of conscience, which is most appropriate when we know we have committed a serious offense (as King David did) or when our lives have exhibited clear patterns of destructive behavior over time and we need regular checks on how our thoughts, feelings, and actions are progressing. Those who turn to twelve-step programs for help with addiction generally become serious about this form of self-examination and know its great value. Recovery spiritualities often take human sin and the need for rigorous self-examination, confession, and restitution more seriously than many churches do.

Yet examination of conscience has value even if we are not aware of needing it. Because we are so adept at hiding the truth of our condition from ourselves as well as from others, it can be a bracing exercise in true humility to look closely at our lives on a regular basis. We begin by asking God to help us see what we need to see about ourselves. Without the Spirit's aid, we cannot penetrate our inner darkness. Our lives are like icebergs; what we know on the surface is a small fraction of what lies below the water level of waking consciousness. The beauty of how God works with us, when we are willing, is that we are enabled by God to see precisely what we need to see and work with.

With the help of God's grace, we begin to search our lives for evidence of "the heart turned in on itself" (Augustine's phrase, based on Paul's letters).

- Where do we feel embarrassed or guilty about what we have done or left undone?
- When have our immediate feelings led us into unkind words or actions?
- Have we allowed others to influence us toward negative judgments of persons we do not really know?
- Do we accept hearsay and gossip without checking facts?
- Where does deceit have a hold on us, and how is it expressed in our lives?

These are examples of the kinds of questions that can help us in a period of examining our conscience. Examination of conscience is an explicitly confessional form of self-examination.

Once we have identified some distorted and damaging habits of our minds and hearts, we can offer a prayer of confession tailored to our personal condition. It is a great release to pour out our heart before God, to whom we can entrust our most vulnerable truths, in trust that God's unreserved love receives us in mercy and yearns to restore to us a wholesome, renewed life. The heart's plea for forgiveness rises from such confession, along with confidence in God's ready willingness to forgive.

Examination of conscience and confession can be wonderfully cathartic, lifting inner burdens that have weighed us down for years. But there is a broader expression of self-examination as well: the examination of consciousness.

PSALM 139 AND EXAMINATION OF CONSCIOUSNESS

Psalm 139 also has the character of self-examination, but it expresses a very different sensibility. First, the psalmist is not so much examining his own faults as marveling that God examines him, inside and out, and knows him completely. There is no direct mention of sin or guilt here, but a keen awareness of being naked before God with no place to hide—an echo, perhaps, of Adam and Eve's condition in the garden after eating the apple. Maybe you remember times as a child when it seemed that your parents could see right through you, and you wondered how they could know what they seemed to know when you were doing your best to conceal it. The sense expressed in this psalm is of being transparent to divine eyes, being encompassed on all sides by a God we cannot escape. But there is ambivalence in the feeling tone—we cannot flee from God's spirit, yet that presence is also comfort and security. At the very farthest limits of human experience, says the psalmist, "your hand shall lead me, and your right hand shall hold me fast" (v. 10). Even darkness is not dark to God, who sees through all obscurity. Whether we experience God's all-penetrating knowledge as comfort or anxiety depends, perhaps, on whether we have something to hide in the darkness or are trying to see something through the darkness.

The psalmist goes on to wonder at how marvelously we are made, how intricate the Creator's weaving of life, and how utterly incomprehensible divine thoughts are. He expresses great appreciation and awe for the gift of human life and form. Then the tone shifts suddenly as he allies himself with God against the wicked who hate God, counting them his own enemies as if to say "I'm on your side, God!" Yet the final verses move back to inward reflection, asking God to search and test his heart for any evil that might be found there and to be led in the way of everlasting life.

This psalm is a beautiful expression of examination of consciousness. If examination of conscience unearths large parts of us in need of total rehabilitation, examination of consciousness helps us to get the bigger picture: the good with the bad.

This examination of consciousness is sometimes simply called the examen, and it is generally practiced at the end of each day. Once again, we come into divine presence seeking the help of the Spirit to see ourselves fully as we are. The focus is on where and when we have experienced God's grace within our day and how we have responded or failed to respond. It is a practice in awareness, an exploration of the contents of our daily consciousness, so that we pay attention to the memorable moments of the day—interactions, situations, activities—and to our inner state in each instance. What were our thoughts, judgments, emotions, beliefs, questions, and observations? Were we conscious of God's presence or prompting in the midst of a conversation, and if so, did we respond in a fitting way? Are we aware in retrospect of how God was indeed with us, but—not catching the grace at the time—how we responded to someone in a less-than-helpful way? Do we have no clue of how or whether God was present in the situation at all?

As we learn to notice our actual thoughts, feelings, and responses in various relationships and circumstances, we may start to become more aware of our physical postures and sensations also. Where do we hold tension in our bodies, and what do those tensions tell us about our reactions? What does our posture tell us about our level of comfort or discomfort, both with ourselves and with others? Slowly, we begin to recognize what lies behind our feelings and reactions; to see whether we are being motivated by self-interest or self-giving; to notice when we are directed by fear or guided by love.

In the process of examen, as we find within us anxiety, hostility, or self-preservation at the expense of others, we are called to confession. We can then seek God's forgiveness and ask for help in seeing more clearly and responding more faithfully next time. And as we discern moments of grace in our day where we responded to others or to our own circumstances with understanding, patience, compassion, or wisdom, we rejoice and give thanks! As Richard Hauser puts it, "On our bad days we are affirmed as forgiven sinners; on our good days we are affirmed as blessed children."[2] There is no way to lose when we open ourselves to a loving God.

In Psalm 139, the psalmist reveals a broad awareness of himself, including the potential for both good and evil. He is conscious of how he has been fearfully and wonderfully made by God's hand. In expressing his marvel at divine handiwork, the psalmist gives us permission to acknowledge gratitude for our God-given goodness as human beings. God does not make anything that is less than wonderful and remarkable, much less anything that is worthless! We have the capacity to live in communion with our Creator and with one another because we are wonderful works of God. And every time we see that we have lived in a way fitting to this purpose, we can celebrate grace.

Toward the end of the psalm, the language changes sharply, expressing intense desire for God to kill the wicked and avowed hatred of all who hate God. Here we are likely to get uncomfortable. The psalmist is surely being very honest, but this is the kind of language used by religious extremists who see God's will in their own hatred of and violence against those they perceive or label as enemies of God. From the standpoint of modern psychology, we might interpret these verses as an unconscious projection of the psalmist's own dark side onto those who do not believe or behave as he does. In our own practice of examen, we should hope to recognize this human tendency in ourselves and, before it becomes too deeply rooted, turn to confession and repentance.

Yet the psalmist, in the end, leaves even these

intensely hard feelings to God's wisdom and judgment. He asks the Lord to search his heart and root out whatever might lead him astray from "the way everlasting." This sorting through feelings and intentions, this self-offering to God's mercy and grace, is the essence of self-examination in both its forms. It is surely what the Sioux tribe in the previous chapter's story committed themselves to work through—each one personally and as a community—in order to freely and truthfully extend themselves as kin to the slayer of one of their own.

Learning forgiveness requires first that we clearly see our own need for it. Self-examination is one of the best ways to discover how deep and ongoing our need truly is. Then we can look more objectively at our urge to judge others, which we will do in the next chapter.

Chapter 3

HONESTY

Engaging the Inner Struggle

Matthew 5:43–48 and 7:1–6

ON ENEMIES AND HONESTY

As we continue to explore the central role of forgiveness in renewing our life and restoring peace, we come to the universal human experience of enmity. We have seen that self-examination helps us stay grounded in the reality of our own need for God's continuing mercy and forgiveness. Only as we become aware of our inner condition can we express ourselves honestly before God. Engaging in a confessional practice like examination of conscience can surface uncomfortable feelings—shame, guilt, anger, and grief. Each of these feelings has a legitimate place in our lives and prayers. Yet because they are intense and we often do not know how to cope with them constructively, we may tend to view them as internal enemies.

Our two basic reactions to enemies are fight and flight. With external enemies, these patterns are more apparent; either we are engaged in audible, tangible combat, or we are avoiding and hiding from the foe. With internal enemies, however, it can be harder to tell if we are fighting or fleeing. We are often unaware of our enmity with disquieting emotions. When inwardly fighting anger, for example, we may subconsciously decide that the easiest way to banish it is to sweep it under the rug. Fighting to keep grief at bay often means trying to convince ourselves and others that we've gotten over it. We typically resist painful, frightening feelings by denying or suppressing them.

We can carry the same strategy into our relationship with external enemies. Since it seems vaguely un-Christian to have bad feelings about anyone, some of us like to imagine that we have no enemies at all. Have you ever said, or heard another say, "I don't have a problem getting along with anyone"?

Difficulty admitting that we have enemies is expressed in the discomfort some Christians feel over portions of the Psalms, especially the so-called imprecatory psalms, which cry out for God's vengeance on perceived enemies. Even doing our best to identify with the Jews in Babylonian captivity, what business do we have as Christians saying, "Happy shall they be who take your little ones and dash them against the rock!" (Ps. 137:9). The Psalms travel widely over the terrain of raw emotion, leaving us uneasy if not queasy. They can descend from heights of glorious praise to depths of vengeful cursing, leaving us dizzy in the wake of sudden mood swings. It's hard to see

the thread of logic leading from eighteen wonder-
struck verses in Psalm 139 to the exclamation, "Do I
not hate those who hate you, O LORD? . . . I hate them
with perfect hatred; I count them my enemies" (vv.
21–22). Just what, Christians might wonder, is perfect
hatred?

Yet the power of the Psalms lies in the permission
they give us to express every conceivable human emotion. Nothing is censored in the intimacy of prayer
with God. But to pray these psalms, we must first get
in touch with aspects of our own experience that cor
respond to the language and emotions of these prayers.
One place to begin is to recognize that we do, in fact,
feel enmity toward certain people. Most of us admit
that there are people in our lives we don't like. It is
harder to acknowledge that there are people—even
whole groups of them—we don't want contact with,
don't want to think about, and certainly don't want to
pray for. They may be people we work or worship with;
figures in government, business, or industry; dictators,
terrorists, or nationalists obsessed with securing power
at the expense of those they consider enemies.

During the Bosnian War, I could barely stand to
think of Radovan Karadzic and Ratko Mladic. But
the events of that time helped me understand psalms I
could not otherwise have imagined praying. For example, I could well imagine a raped Muslim woman praying the first six verses of Psalm 94:

Yahweh, God of revenge,
God of revenge, appear!
Rise, judge of the world,
give the proud their desserts!

Yahweh, . . .
how much longer are the wicked to triumph?
Are these evil men to remain unsilenced,
boasting and asserting themselves?

Yahweh, they crush your people,
they oppress your hereditary people,
murdering and massacring
widows, orphans and guests.

Jerusalem Bible

With victims of random slaughter from Rwanda to
Darfur, I have at times found myself praying the invec-
tive against brute force found in Psalm 69:22–28:

May their own table prove a trap for them,
and their plentiful supplies, a snare!
May their eyes grow dim, go blind,
strike their loins with chronic palsy!

Vent your fury on them,
let your burning anger overtake them;
may their camp be reduced to ruin,
and their tents left unoccupied:
. . . .

Charge them with crime after crime,
. . . .
blot them out of the book of life.

Jerusalem Bible

If I can admit that my heart fights to keep certain
people outside the boundaries of my love, I can at least
begin asking God to help me stretch those boundaries.
The way I typically pray for brutal autocrats or terrorists is to ask God to convert them: "Dear Lord, please
confront these dreadful people with their colossal self-
delusion, paranoia, and lust for power." But then I am

really asking God to confirm my judgment of these people. Perhaps this is only a bit more civilized than baldly praying against my enemy, a tactic admirably illustrated by Texas Ranger Captain Jack Hays just before the battle of Palo Alto in the Mexican-American War: "O Lord, we are about to join battle with vastly superior numbers of the enemy, and . . . we would mightily like for you to be on our side. . . . But if you can't do it, . . . just lie low . . . , and You will see one of the dangest fights you've ever seen. Charge!"[1]

Jesus teaches, "Love your enemies and pray for those who persecute you" (Matt. 5:44). Church historian Glenn Hinson suggests that sometimes the only way to love our enemies is to pray for them. Hinson speaks from experience, having suffered persecution at the hands of ruthless fundamentalists. I have certainly found it to be true that we cannot continue to despise a person for whom we regularly and sincerely pray. Hinson confesses that he doesn't find it easy to pray for those who revile him: "Imprecatory psalms have a job to do before I get to the point that I can pray *for* my enemies. I'll have to release some anger first and let God do something with it that I can't."[2]

When we release pain and anger to God over people who seem impossible to embrace with love, the Spirit begins a mysterious process in our hearts. God reveals to us the enemy within our own divided self— the wounded, scary aspects of ourselves we have tried so hard to ignore, the sides of us that are humiliating to admit. Each of us secretly harbors despised parts of our own personality, impulses and reactions we are ashamed of: jealousy, greed, rage, self-pity, the need to be right, the desire to win, the exhilaration of feeling superior. These aspects of our character embarrass us when they come to light. They also signal our potential for seriously injuring others as well as ourselves. Have we never rationalized a selfish motive as something good? Never twisted the truth just a little to preserve our own advantage or to save face? Have we never tried to co-opt God into the service of our own favorite cause or limited ideology? How far might we go if we felt sufficiently pressured by peers or personally threatened?

Mother Teresa of Calcutta was once asked why she did what she did. She replied that it was because she knew that a little Hitler lived inside her. To her admirers such a response may sound like hyperbole, but it is consistent with the witness of all great saints, who are acutely conscious of their capacity for sin. Only by God's grace do we escape falling, and only by grace can we do what is truly good.

JUDGMENT AND EGO

When we begin to see ourselves standing with those who have fallen into the seduction of sin—to see, at least, that we are more like them than we are like God—it casts a whole new light on what it means to pray for our enemies. We can stand under God's judgment with them, we can implore God's mercy for all of us, but we can no longer simply stand in judgment over against them. We begin to see why judgment is God's prerogative, and not ours, and why we are bidden to forgive one another as God has forgiven us.

Our need to judge others is largely a function of the ego, our false and fallen self. Recall that the ego creates its own kingdom in which everything revolves around it as the center. This little realm of illusions is largely unconscious, for the ego thrives best in the dark. It hides its true motives and intentions from our consciousness so that we do not readily see its seductions and manipulations. Whenever we start to become aware of its operations, say through self-examination, the ego will feel threatened. It will devise one strategy after another to throw us off course as we search for greater self-awareness. The ego knows that when it is fully exposed to the light of day it will die, or at least it will lose much of its power to shape our lives.

The early desert abbas and ammas (spiritual fathers and mothers of the fourth through sixth centuries) understood how central human judgments were to our false self and what a struggle it was to let them go. Many of their sayings address our habits of judging others. Here is one story told of Abba Moses, a great father of fourth-century Egypt:

> A brother at Scetis committed a fault. A council was called to which Abba Moses was invited, but he refused to go to it. Then the priest sent someone to say to him, "Come, for everyone is waiting for you." So he got up and went. He took a leaking jug, filled it with water and carried it with him. The others came out to meet him and said to him, "What is this, Father?" The old man said to them, "My sins run out behind me, and I do not see them, and today I am coming to judge the errors of another." When they heard that they said no more to the brother but forgave him.[3]

Abba Moses notes that he does not see the sins running out behind him. He knows well how unconscious we are concerning our own faults. It is much easier to see others' faults than our own, because the ego leads us to hide and rationalize our dark side. Jesus addresses this side of human behavior in the Sermon on the Mount: "Why do you see the speck in your neighbor's eye, but do not notice the log in your own eye?" (7:3). There is humor in Jesus' hyperbole: If we would just take the log out of our own eye, we might actually be able to see clearly enough to remove the speck from our neighbor's!

We get ourselves in trouble when we begin measuring the relative "weight" of human sins. To whatever extent other people's sins seem obviously greater than our own, we may let ourselves more easily off the hook. We feel justified in regarding with shock and horror the "big sins" of others, effectively keeping eyes off our own sins and allowing us to feel a certain measure of self-righteousness. The desert Christians had something to say about this tactic:

> Abba Theodore also said, "If you are temperate, do not judge the fornicator, for you would then transgress the law just as much. And he who said, 'Do not commit fornication,' also said, 'Do not judge.'"[4]

In other words, the very act of judging another human being puts us at odds with Christ's command. At the moment we judge another person, we become liable to God's judgment ourselves: "For with the judgment you make you will be judged" (7:2). It does not matter how great or small a sin appears to us. We cannot know that God's view of the magnitude of a given sin will match our view of that sin, because God alone knows the particular struggles of each person's soul.

The desert abbas and ammas were adamant about this point: Our human task is to observe clearly, admit to, and repent of our own sins. It is folly for one sinner to judge another.

This is a very difficult perspective for us to grasp and may well be one we do not agree with. After all, the Ten Commandments seem to elevate certain sins above others, and the legal code of the Torah specifies different degrees of punishment for various infractions of the law. The institutional church has historically distinguished between mortal sins and venial sins, and our modern justice system makes distinctions between major and minor criminal offenses. The idea that judging the sins of another is as sinful as the other's actual sins deeply challenges our notions of justice.

Then again, Jesus' teachings often challenged people to stretch beyond conventional understandings of law, justice, and custom. Jesus was constantly being accused by religious leaders of transgressing laws, especially Sabbath laws. The teachers of Judaism were both repelled and fascinated by Jesus' relationship to the law. They tested him to see how he would respond to the Jewish law about stoning adulterers caught in the act, or whether he believed Roman laws levying taxes on Jews were legitimate. Jesus had a maddening way of eluding conventional responses and categories of thinking.

CONDEMNATION OR DISCERNMENT?

As we try to sort out what we believe concerning judgment, let's note that the word carries two basic meanings: condemnation and discernment. When we speak of someone exercising good judgment, we mean it in the sense of useful discrimination or discerning perception. Discernment is the positive face of judgment. Jesus told his disciples to be "wise as serpents and innocent as doves" (10:16). The wisdom of the serpent is a metaphor for worldly discernment, suggesting a measure of judicious craftiness. Perhaps it implies a certain practical detachment as well, such as in Jesus' counsel to his disciples to shake the dust off their feet when leaving towns that did not respond to their message (10:14) or in his words to listeners not to "throw your pearls before swine" (7:6). Notice that this counsel comes immediately after Jesus' warning against judging others! Perhaps practical discretion about where to give your energies, and to whom, expresses discerning judgment and fits the idea of being wise as serpents.

The judgments of condemnation are something very different. Condemnation is the negative face of judgment. Jesus has hard words about this sort of condemning attitude early in his Sermon on the Mount. He indicates that when we are angry with a sister or brother, we make ourselves liable to judgment, and if we insult others or call them fools, we subject ourselves to divine wrath (5:21–22). Jesus is explicitly telling us that angry attitudes and condemning insults are just as spiritually dangerous as murder.

The problem with judging the offenses of others is that we fall straight into our own offenses. It is one of many ways that we become like our enemies in attempting to fight them.

There is another way, however—a third way beyond fight or flight, beyond denial of the enmity inside us or resistance to the enemy outside. It is the way the Sioux tribe took in making a new relation of one who had deprived them of a relation. It is the way Jesus took on the cross to reconcile hostile, confused human beings with God. It is the way of love. Henri Nouwen spoke of forgiveness as love's name in a wounded world. In the next chapter, we will explore more fully the meaning of such love in our lives.

Chapter 4

REPENTANCE

Getting a New Mind

Luke 23:32–43

GOD'S LOVE AND JUDGMENT

As we ponder the role forgiveness plays in a renewed life of peace, we come inevitably to the theme of love. The way of love, God's way, offers us a third alternative to our reactive habits of fight and flight when we are injured or offended by others. This path is embodied for us in the life and death of Jesus Christ. In him we see clearly how God chooses to relate to us when we offend against the divine heart, violating the communion of love that God intended for us in creation. Breaking the communion of love with God and one another is the fundamental human sin in need of healing and reconciliation. Divine forgiveness is critical to restoring this relationship.

How, then, are we to square God's forgiveness
and God's judgment? The Bible is full of pictures of
divine judgment, both past and promised. While Jesus
warns us about the hypocrisy of judging others when
we ourselves stand under judgment, he never suggests
that judgment is inappropriate for God. Indeed, the
Scriptures are clear that only God, in whom there is no
shadow of unrighteousness, has the right to judge and
condemn human sin. How do we reconcile divine judgment with divine love?

In beholding Jesus on the cross, we see how God
chooses to hold the tension between these polarities.
The cross itself is a dreadful judgment against humanity. It stands as witness to our brutality against innocent human beings, our will to destroy truth-tellers in
order to preserve our illusions of power, control, and
rightness. The choice of the crowds to crucify a contro-
versial spiritual teacher reflects a reality we see played
out repeatedly in human history: pushing God's truth
to the margins of human consciousness in favor of the
self-congratulatory mind-set of "me, mine, and my
kind."

The Holy One does not deny justice in response
to our sin; nor does the All-Merciful force us to pay a
price beyond our means, since we are incapable by ourselves of restoring the damage we cause. God neither
obliterates us in divine retribution (fight) nor retreats
into sentimental acceptance of our faults without consequences (flight). Instead, God's justice and love are
fused into a single response and a singular invitation.
As the Word made flesh, Jesus takes divine judgment
into his own body on our behalf. He re-presents our

humanity before God, receiving divine justice for sin, and he re-presents God to us, offering divine forgiveness for sin. God-in-Christ is willing to pay this price; a just love costs dearly. Jesus Christ is the embodied paradox of divine love and justice, revealing God's grace as a form of judgment and offering God's judgment in the form of grace. Judgment without mercy is brutal; mercy without judgment is anemic. God holds the balance in a love beyond comprehension, incarnate in Christ.

The singular invitation for us is to join God's project of redemption, to participate in this quality of divine love as long as sin endures. For there is something that endures more surely than sin: Love "bears all things, believes all things, hopes all things, endures all things" (1 Cor. 13:7). Nothing but love is finally capable of bearing or enduring all things. This is the great hope and promise of our faith—that God's love will outlast every form of opposition, that the forces of darkness within and beyond us will finally relent and recognize that "Christ is all and in all" (Col. 3:11).

How do we learn to live inside this quality of love, this holy hope and patient persistence? Christian philosopher Blaise Pascal famously said, "Jesus will be in agony until the end of the world."[1] When we consider that what we do to the least of our brothers or sisters we do to Christ (Matt. 25:40), and when we observe what we as human beings actually do to one another generation upon generation, we must recognize that God's redemption is a work in progress as well as a gift given for all time. It is already but not yet, to borrow the phrase often used to describe our situation between

Christ's first and second coming. How do we participate in God's ongoing redemption of a world awash in
self-absorption?

THE SPIRIT OF REPENTANCE

As we have already seen, our first task is to seek to
extricate ourselves from that self-absorption. The first
order of business is not to forgive others but to receive
the forgiveness God offers us in the agonizingly out-
stretched arms of Christ on the cross. Exploring self-
examination and our need for confession has moved us
in this direction. Looking hard at our human impulse
to judge and acknowledging our need to attend to our
own faults has taken us a step further. We have yet to
explore the deeper spirit of repentance, one of the key
practices of Lent.

The word used most consistently for repentance in
the New Testament is *metanoia*. It is a combination of
the Greek words *meta*, which means "beyond," and
nous, or "mind." Repentance means adopting a new
mind-set, going beyond our ordinary ways of thinking,
perceiving, and responding to life. Our ordinary mind-
set is shaped by our little ego kingdoms and typically
takes one of two forms: Either we proudly trust in our
own mental or physical powers to meet life, thinking
of ourselves as self-made people who can figure out
our own problems and do things right by sheer inven-
tiveness and grit, or we fearfully distrust that we have
any real good in us, despairing of personal power to
meet life's challenges and indulging in self-pity. But the
inflated self and the deflated self are merely two sides

of the same coin: ego. In the realm of ego, each personal universe revolves endlessly around an inadequate picture of selfhood.

The purpose of repentance is to transcend our limited view of reality. The word *metanoia* suggests that opening up to God's much larger and more generous view of reality requires us at some level to go "out of our minds"—at least as they now operate. Our self-absorbed mind-set is intent on finding those things all people yearn for: security, affirmation, recognition, love, and meaning. But the blinders of ego-need have us looking for these things in all the wrong places: material possessions, status, honors, insider knowledge, and gratification of physical appetites, to name the most obvious. The sad truth we discover only with time is that none of these sources of presumed security or fulfillment have the ability to satisfy our hearts.

Repentance, then, involves turning ourselves in a new direction: away from ego and toward God. Disillusionment with our self-made efforts to find life's satisfaction is a wonderful prompt. The beginning of repentance is putting ourselves in God's hands, acknowledging that we need what only our Creator can give. Slowly we begin to see that God has already given us an identity far more precious than what the world promises. Spiritually speaking, we are children of the Most High, beloved sons and daughters, brothers and sisters equally made in the image of God. Each of us is a unique constellation of personhood, designed to reflect the divine likeness in our own way. What could be more astonishingly wonderful?

Repentance brings us to genuine sorrow over all

the energy of our lives wasted in grasping for illusory things, all the time dissipated in failing to seek God's ready help, guidance, and love. True repentance carries this sadness along with a powerful desire to change, knowing that in reality we can open ourselves to being changed only by a power beyond our own. We groan inwardly with the psalmist, "Create in me a clean heart, O God, and put a new and right spirit within me" (Ps. 51:10). Without authentic sorrow and desire to be "clothed and in [our] right mind" (Mark 5:15), acts of contrition are but external shows. These same principles shape our repentance when we seek restored relationship with one another.

SEEKING FORGIVENESS FROM OTHERS

When, through self-examination, we become honest about our weaknesses, about our pride and fear, about our part in the sordid affairs of the human family, we can begin to notice the people in our lives we have misjudged and mistreated. We start to see faces: those we have made no effort to understand, those we have ignored or avoided, those we have been jealous of, those to whom we have not kept our promises, those we have criticized or belittled. Most of our ways of wounding each other are emotional. We withhold acceptance, affirmation, personal warmth; we exclude and reject; we betray trust and gossip behind backs; we make snide comments, dish out criticism, and harp on weaknesses; we even shame publicly and play games of emotional blackmail, threatening to expose another's secrets in order to gain what we want. Sometimes we hurt each other without meaning to, simply by being inattentive or self-absorbed.

As we become convinced that we need to seek forgiveness from those we have injured, oppressed, or offended, the same principles apply that are central to restoring our relationship with God. Our sorrow for what we have done or failed to do must be real. Our desire to see someone in a new way and respond with a more generous spirit must also be genuine.

If it is possible to go directly to the person we have injured, the potential for reconciliation is greatest. If direct contact is not feasible, a letter can be a fine way to reach out. In situations where we cannot bring ourselves to make contact directly, we can ask a mutual friend or third party to make an overture on our behalf. When the offended person responds receptively, we should not delay our follow-up contact. Even when the first overture is less than enthusiastically received, it is up to us to try again. Strong resolve and persistence helps the offended party to see that we are serious in seeking forgiveness and reconciliation.

This brings us to the matter of apology. It can feel remarkably hard to apologize to someone, even for a relatively minor offense. To apologize requires an admission of being wrong. This is humbling, but if our apology is genuine, we will need to prepare ourselves to accept a certain level of embarrassment with ourselves and before the other person. Inevitably we feel a certain loss of power and control when we humble ourselves this way. Indeed, the self-humbling is part of what makes an apology effective.

According to Carl Schneider, a mediation specialist, there are three essential components in a good apology:

- *Acknowledging a particular offense and being willing to take responsibility for it.* This involves admitting that real injury was done, that a relationship was damaged in some way—in dignity, respect, or trust. It also involves saying, "I did this."
- *Showing a visible feeling of regret or shame.* This makes it clear to the offended party that the offender is personally affected by what she or he did and is troubled by it: "I am sorry for what I did, and I regret the suffering I caused."
- *Being vulnerable to the offended party.* This means offering no defense of oneself, standing exposed and vulnerable to the response of the offended person. An apology is offered with no guarantee of acceptance; forgiveness may be begged for and refused.[2]

The power of apology lies in "the exchange of shame and power between the offender and the offended," says Aaron Lazare.[3] A role reversal takes place: Whereas in the original injury the offender had power and the offended felt shame, in the apology the offender feels shame and the offended assumes power. An apology is thus a ritual of moral rebalancing.

What makes for a bad apology?

- *Not fully acknowledging the injury done or not taking direct responsibility:* "If some of what I said was disrespectful, . . ." "Mistakes were made." "I'm

sorry if you felt hurt by what I did." This last
tactic subtly places blame back on the offended
and implies that he or she had some level of
unjustified temerity to feel hurt by what you
did—that the problem is less what you did than
how the other person reacted.

– *Not expressing sorrow or shame,* a lapse illustrated
in President Clinton's now-classic nonapology
for the Lewinsky affair. Body language and tone
of voice can also betray lack of authentic feelings of remorse. If it appears that we are more
sorry for getting caught than for what we did
and how it affected others, then the apology
falls flat.

– *Defending ourselves.* Any form of self-justification
erases the effectiveness of an apology. The more
excuses we build into an "apology," the more
apparent it becomes that we have basically exon-
erated ourselves already. A good apology is brief,
to the point, and heartfelt, with no explanations
or rationalizations.

RECEIVING FORGIVENESS

We make ourselves vulnerable with others in seeking forgiveness, never knowing whether our sincerest
efforts will be met with mercy. If we do not receive
forgiveness, we need to wait patiently in hope, praying that an opening will come in God's time. If the
offended person offers forgiveness, we should receive
it humbly and gratefully, with an inward commitment

not to fall into such injurious behavior again. To ask for and then receive forgiveness is a healing balm, usually for both parties. It is a heavy emotional burden lifted from us that we need not carry again.

When we seek forgiveness from God with genuine repentance, we can rest assured by faith that forgiveness is granted. We need not feel anxious or uncertain about God's response, as we might with other persons. This is the good news! The only response we can make to this ever available but very costly grace is to receive it with trusting gratitude and to commit ourselves with every ounce of our intention to avoid this fault in the future with the help of the Spirit.

Receiving divine forgiveness, though, is not always as simple or straightforward as it might seem. We sometimes "take back our sin" to fondle or replay it. If we have learned to depend on destructive behavior for a sense of identity, even a negative identity, it will be hard to let go. At other times, we can't quite believe that God would forgive certain sins or truly love us unconditionally. Like Groucho Marx proclaiming, "I don't care to belong to any club that will accept me as a member," we basically say, "I wouldn't believe in a God who could love me as I am or forgive me after what I've done." In doing so, we are holding up higher standards than God's for our forgiveness, a rather arrogant posture for all its apparent humility. When we find that we have not truly forgiven ourselves for an injury we caused, we can be sure that we have not yet fully received the forgiveness God extends. The blockage is on our side, not God's.

We can only give what we have already received. If

we wish to participate in the generous outpouring of God's love and forgiveness for a wounded world, we need to receive it fully and know from experience both its grace and cost. Divine love—the way beyond fight or flight—stands its ground. It has nothing to prove and nothing to hide. It may be accepted or rejected, but it will not on either account lose its character: It endures. When we take God's love into our hearts, we have firm ground on which to stand when it comes our turn to forgive others—our subject for the next chapter.

Chapter 5

FORGIVING

Embracing Freedom

Matthew 18:23–35

THE CALL TO FORGIVE

We know we are bidden to forgive one another as God, in Christ, has forgiven us. It is difficult to miss all the references in the Gospels to this basic expression of the Christian calling. We find it at the heart of the Lord's Prayer: "And forgive us our sins, for we ourselves forgive everyone indebted to us" (Luke 11:4). It is embedded in Jesus' teaching on judging others in Luke's Gospel: "Do not judge, and you will not be judged; do not condemn, and you will not be condemned. Forgive, and you will be forgiven" (6:37). Jesus uses hyperbole to respond to Peter's question about how many times he should forgive a church member who sins against him. Peter assumes that seven times would be generous, but

Jesus explodes his calculus: "Not seven times, but, I tell you, seventy-seven times" (Matt. 18:22)—sometimes translated "seventy times seven," a number yet more unimaginable to Peter. Paul also urges forgiveness as a basic Christian virtue: "Bear with one another and, if anyone has a complaint against another, forgive each other; just as the Lord has forgiven you, so you also must forgive" (Col. 3:13).

Nowhere do we find a more arresting depiction of the reason for forgiving our fellows than in Jesus' parable of the Unforgiving Servant (Matt. 18:23–35). This parable would be striking enough, and much easier to swallow, without the final two verses. The king is the figure of God in this cautionary tale, and each of us is invited to see ourselves in the unforgiving servant. It is critical to understand the monetary sums in this story, or the point will have far less force to modern readers than it had for Jesus' hearers. A denarius was the customary daily wage for a common laborer, making the smaller debt worth about three and a half months of labor. A talent was worth more than fifteen years of ordinary wages; ten thousand talents would represent a debt beyond 150,000 years of common labor, an astronomical sum by any standard. Jesus' point is that we owe God vastly more than what anyone could possibly owe us. His parable strongly implies that God has already forgiven us this unbearable debt and expects us in turn to forgive the far smaller debts of others. Moreover, Jesus is uncomfortably direct about the destructive consequences of failing to forgive others.

The sense in most New Testament teachings is that forgiving others is imperative, not optional. Jesus is

not merely inviting or suggesting forgiveness. Spiritually speaking, we are obliged to forgive one another.
This is easier said than done, of course, as illustrated
by another story from early desert wisdom:

> Certain of the brethren said to Abba Anthony: We
> would like you to tell us some word, by which we
> may be saved. Then the elder said: You have heard
> the Scriptures, they ought to be enough for you. But
> they said: We want to hear something also from you,
> Father. The elder answered them: You have heard
> the Lord say: If a man strikes you on the left cheek,
> show him also the other one. They said to him: This
> we cannot do. He said to them: If you can't turn the
> other cheek, at least take it patiently on one of them.
> They replied: We can't do that either. He said: If you
> cannot even do that, at least do not go striking others
> more than you would want them to strike you. They
> said: We cannot do this either. Then the elder said to
> his disciple: Go cook up some food for these brethren,
> for they are very weak. Finally he said to them: If you
> cannot even do this, how can I help you? All I can do
> is pray.[1]

Surely this humorous story elicits some chuckles or
groans of recognition in us. Our weakness is rooted in
both human emotion and our reasoned sense of justice
as "fair play." In this chapter, we will look more closely
at human emotion as a roadblock to forgiveness. In the
next chapter, we will examine our notions of justice in
relation to forgiveness and consider various forms of
justice.

Normal human feelings can easily block our acting
on the knowledge that forgiveness is imperative for followers of Christ. Such feelings can abort even our desire
to forgive. In my own experience, I would distinguish

between two basic types of emotional response: (1) "I should but I don't want to," and (2) "I can't yet."

WHEN I DON'T WANT TO FORGIVE

In this first instance, there is a distinct element of satisfaction in feeling resentment when such resentment may be easily justified. Feeling wounded or offended is generally sufficient justification. These feelings are often based in ego needs. We enjoy a certain amount of complaining to others about how unjustly we have been treated. It can be a good exercise in self-examination to ask how much of what we feel is legitimate and how much makes a juicy-good story of victimhood to elicit sympathy from others.

Let me illustrate with my own experience of job loss. Several years ago, I was told that the organization for which I'd worked for nearly thirteen years was cutting my position due to economic constraints. The news came as a terrible shock. I had thought my work central and valuable enough to warrant more effort to keep me on staff. At one level, I felt aggrieved and victimized. It seemed the work I had done was devalued, and I felt the sting of realizing that I was far from indispensable to the organization. These were simply blows to my ego. I could easily have wallowed in the seductions of feeling unjustly dismissed, knowing that many of my colleagues were shocked and dismayed by what had happened to me. Their sympathy at times fueled my sense of entitlement to my feelings of resentment.

Thankfully, I was aware early on that these feelings were ego-derived and ego-driven. When I was honest with myself, a much larger picture held sway. God was simply closing a door that I had seriously pondered walking through myself for more than two years. My soul was no longer fully engaged with the position I had held for more than a decade. I had known it was time to move on but had not had the courage to walk away from a good salary with benefits in a weakening economy. In this larger picture, the Holy Spirit was pushing me out of my comfortable nest and into a freedom I had been craving for years. That the decision was made for me rather than by me was simply part of the embarrassment I had to come to terms with. Additionally, I was well aware of the financial stress our organization was under and knew my position would not have been cut if my boss had seen a good alternative. There was no animosity behind the decision; rather, there was much agonizing and regret.

As long as I focused on "what they did to me," I placed myself in the victim stance, where resentment felt justified. But the moment I lifted my eyes to the divine initiative that I could see so clearly behind surface facts, I no longer felt aggrieved but relieved! That put me in a posture where forgiveness scarcely seemed relevant. Painful as it was to be torn away from a community of colleagues, and as anxiety-provoking as the loss of steady income was, I could thank my boss for cutting the strings of organizational constraint and setting me loose to explore my calling afresh.

Perhaps my experience can raise questions concerning the larger perspective from which we choose to see and respond to life's circumstances. How do we see a situation when we step away from our egos? How broad or high is our perspective, and what might God's perception be? What new possibilities lie within the pain of the moment? What new life sleeps inside this form of death, waiting to be wakened? Our capacity to explore such questions will depend in part on the nature of the offense, the depth of the wound experienced, and the level of our own emotional and spiritual maturity.

WHEN I CAN'T YET FORGIVE

There are times when our truthful response to the call to forgive is "I can't yet." If my job loss had created a serious financial crisis for our family, I might well have needed more time to acknowledge and absorb the larger positive picture. Had I not known my soul was already seeking another horizon, forgiveness would no doubt have proved more of a challenge. "I can't yet" is a perfectly honest and reasonable response and may even be the healthiest response under some circumstances.

In situations where persons have experienced repeated abuse—physical or emotional—the abuser can be forgiven too quickly to have any benefit either to the abuser or the abused. Abusers routinely show remorse and ask for forgiveness, only to repeat their behavior the next time their need for control is threatened. Forgiveness then becomes a meaningless ritual, providing little more than psychological cover for abusers to continue their destructive behavior. They learn to assume that the abused will forgive them, so they can resume the cycle of violence from a "clean slate."

Receiving forgiveness glibly, their attitude echoes Voltaire's reputed comment: "I like to sin, God likes to forgive, really the world is admirably arranged."

Serious offenses against the humanity of a person involving physical or psychological trauma cannot be forgiven quickly. When we are deeply wounded by betrayal or violence, it will take time, perhaps a long time, before sufficient inner healing prepares the soil of our hearts to nurture the fruit of forgiveness. When a loss is irreversible, when trust has been shattered and the heart battered, when fear is intense and grief overwhelming, we should not expect ourselves to leap easily to forgiveness. In most cases there will be layers of psychological excavation, inner healing, and the hard work of spiritual practice before forgiveness can be authentic for us.

STORIES OF FORGIVENESS

On the other hand, there are countless stories of deeply traumatized people who found it within their hearts to extend forgiveness to brutal offenders. There was Kelly, whose fiancé revealed shortly before their wedding that he had been dishonest with her about his past and consequently could not marry her. She was crushed. Yet thirty years later, still single, she was well beyond bitterness and self-pity. Though he never showed remorse, Kelly fully forgave him and found fulfillment in serving others. Then there was Chris. At age ten he was kidnapped, stabbed, and shot by a man who was angry with Chris's father. Twenty-two years later, Chris encountered his attacker, who was in a local nursing home—frail, blind, and in ruined health. On learning the identity of his visitor, the ailing man expressed his deep regret at what he had done to Chris as a child. Chris responded by offering both forgiveness and friendship until the day the old man died.

Stories like these are not as rare as we might imagine. We are resilient creatures, capable of throwing off shackles of bitterness and discovering more about ourselves and others over time. The impetus to forgive sometimes comes from sheer fatigue at carrying the burden of anger and resentment. We begin to see that rage, grief, and lust for retaliation can easily trap us in a self-imposed prison of hate that corrodes our soul's energy and peace. At some point, we discover the self-interest of renewed personal well-being in the act of forgiving our offenders. Choosing to forgive is one of the most freeing and healing choices we can make in life.

The therapeutic value of forgiving others is perhaps good enough reason to strive for this virtue, but less self-interested reasons surface in many stories we encounter. The freedom to forgive often comes from discovering the humanity of the offender, even violent offenders. Chris could see the vulnerability of his childhood attacker, a man without family or friends in his last years of life, companioned only by regret. The young man found his residual fear dissolving and his natural compassion aroused. Ron, the brother of a victim of the infamous "pickax murderer" Karla Faye Tucker, eventually discovered the human being behind this dreadful act. Karla's drug-addicted prostitute mother introduced her daughter to drugs, sex, and prostitution when Karla was very young. She was high on drugs when she committed the murders. Only in jail did someone introduce her to the Bible and give her something to begin to live for. Ron recognized aspects of his own difficult life in Karla's and, eventually, through a remarkable transformation of his own heart, formed a prison friendship with his sister's killer. At the scene of Karla's execution, Ron was not in the witness room set up for victim's families where he could have been, but in the near-empty room for the family of the condemned.[2]

Stories like these can give us courage and inspiration to see that forgiveness is possible even in the direst situations. In most cases, they involve a long period of struggle and healing. Help from trained third parties can often reduce the length of such struggle. Therapists and spiritual directors may help a person move through phases of anger and grief more effectively or to see a larger picture of good coming from evil. Trained mediators can also help people gain new perspective, especially where both parties in a dispute feel wounded and aggrieved, as is often the case with troubled marriages. In some instances, mediators can help a crime victim encounter the offender in a way that keeps the victim safe and allows the offender to express regret. Seeking such mediation early can help reduce the period of trauma for the victim.

One remarkable story of mediation and the courage of two men to engage it fully may help illustrate the value of this kind of assistance. During a motel robbery, a young man named Wayne shot Gary, the fellow working behind the front desk, at point-blank range. Gary survived but suffered from physical and psychological scars for many years. He finally decided the only way to find healing from recurrent nightmares and posttraumatic stress was to confront his attacker. He contacted a mediation program that arranged for a face-to-face meeting between the two men at the prison where Wayne was held.

Once the men were seated across a table from each other, a mediator placed them on equal footing rather than reinforcing roles such as "victim" and "perpetrator." He began by asking both men to look at each other and to talk to each other as "human beings, man to man." Empowered with trust in their basic humanity, the two men proceeded. Gary politely, but with a shaky voice, asked Wayne to explain why the robbery had gotten so violent. He also described how his life had never been the same and how his family and work had been affected by the trauma of being shot. Wayne, faced directly with the human impact of his actions, said repeatedly how sorry he was for what he had done and how it had affected Gary and his family. Each man was able to recognize and acknowledge that the other had lost much in the aftermath of this violence. Both were empowered with new understanding of the other and of themselves. Gary received Wayne's apology and thanked him for it, which helped Wayne feel accepted, inwardly freed, and taken seriously as a person. The exchange was transformative. Gary came to Wayne's parole hearing and asked for his release. Since then, they have appeared many times throughout New York State to speak of their experience.[3]

Did Gary forgive Wayne? The dialogue between them does not explicitly contain forgiveness. Yet because the conditions of reconciliation were met, Gary's forgiveness of Wayne was strongly implied in their interaction and subsequent relationship. Connections and distinctions between forgiveness and reconciliation are well worth clarifying. In the final chapter, we will look at this relationship and how it fits with our notions of fair play and justice.

Chapter 6

BEGINNING AGAIN

Reconciliation and Restoration

Luke 7:36–47

FORGIVENESS AND RECONCILIATION

The story of Gary and Wayne from the last chapter raises some interesting questions about the relationship between forgiveness and reconciliation. Is it possible to be reconciled to someone without forgiveness? Does forgiveness lead naturally to reconciliation? Are we still obliged by Christian principle to forgive if no reconciliation seems possible?

The conversation between Gary and Wayne did not contain the language of forgiveness directly. It was rich with the language of apology in the best sense: Wayne took full responsibility for what he had done to Gary, did not try to justify or rationalize his violent act, and apologized with sincere feeling several times for the suffering and loss it had caused Gary and his family over many years. In turn, Gary treated Wayne respectfully, accepted his apology with gratitude, and acknowledged that Wayne had also sustained great loss from his act, namely, freedom and opportunity.

In this ritual of heartfelt apology offered and received, the balance of shame and power was reversed (from attacker having power and victim having shame, to attacker having shame and victim having power). The moral order of their human relationship was symbolically rebalanced, opening the door to reconciliation. Such rebalancing is one expression of justice. In the case of Gary and Wayne, the process allowed them to achieve reconciliation. These two men, who had no previous relationship except through the chance of random crime, came to a sufficient understanding of each other that they chose to share publicly with others their experience of mediation and the healing it had brought to each of their lives.

More ordinary instances of reconciliation without apparent forgiveness can often be found in family life. My mother-in-law grew up in a dysfunctional family and was estranged from her younger sister for decades. Late in life, circumstances brought the two sisters together again, and they had a very pleasant visit. My mother-in-law said simply that they never talked about the past. Their restored connection lasted until her sister's death at a ripe old age. What happened here? I suspect that the two sisters were weary of old family feuds and, conscious of the fragility of life, wanted nothing more than to know one another as sisters again. They had no desire to rehash the past and perhaps feared that raising old issues would bring back bad feelings. No acknowledgments or apologies were part of this reconciliation, only a mutual desire to start the relationship anew.

I believe that a basic level of forgiveness is implied wherever genuine reconciliation occurs. It may not be spoken, but the inner attitude allowing for reconciliation involves a certain letting go of the past, at least releasing how one has chosen to perceive and relate to the other person in the past. We might say that a forgiving heart, or at least an open-minded attitude toward the future, is a necessary part of any true reconciliation.

Forgiveness does not, however, always lead to reconciliation. We are complex creatures, full of illusions and inward resistance to what could bring new life. Just as an offended person may not accept the offender's apology, an offender may not take in the forgiveness given by the offended. Suppose Wayne had offered his apology and Gary had responded with a direct statement of forgiveness, but Wayne, acutely uncomfortable with such forgiveness, had retreated into a shell of shame. Until Wayne could forgive himself and accept Gary's gift, no real reconciliation could occur between them.

Forgiveness and reconciliation are two steps along a continuum. Reconciliation is the larger goal, reflecting the divine aim for our relationships with others and with God, but it is not always possible for us to achieve reconciliation with others in this life. The offender may be dead, in a coma, living in an undisclosed location, or never even positively identified as the perpetrator.

Sometimes the culprit does not think anything needs to be forgiven: "That's your problem not mine." "I'm sorry if you felt that what I did was a problem, but I don't see it that way."

When reconciliation seems impossible, we are left with a choice about whether or not to move forward with forgiveness on our side. Forgiving can be, and often is, a one-way street. But to accept our full freedom to forgive unilaterally may mean navigating around the obstacle of our felt need for the other's repentance and our cherished ideas of justice and fair play.

REPENTANCE AND FORGIVENESS

Many people believe that forgiveness is not possible without repentance, and that to offer it before repentance is a travesty of just, accountable relationships. This is the classic Jewish posture on forgiveness, and we see it reflected in many biblical texts from both Hebrew and Christian sources. The early legal codes of Israel are clear about how to handle sins such as lying, robbery, and fraud: The person responsible must first acknowledge guilt for specific sins, then pay restitution of equal value plus one-fifth (presumably a "punitive damage") to the person sinned against, and finally give a guilt offering (unblemished animal) to the priest to make atonement before God for sin (see Lev. 6:1–7 and Num. 5:5–7). Then, and only then, is forgiveness granted. Confession and restitution are concrete signs of repentance.

The sequence of sin, repentance, and forgiveness is our cultural norm. We relate to the basic pattern in Psalm 51, where the psalmist confesses his sin, acknowledges his transgression, and begs God to create in him a clean heart and restore him to the joy of salvation. The sacrifice here is not an animal but "a broken and contrite heart." We understand Jesus' words in Luke 17:3–4: "If another disciple sins, you must rebuke the offender, and if there is repentance, you must forgive. And if the same person sins against you seven times a day, and turns back to you seven times and says, 'I repent,' you must forgive." At least this makes more sense to us than Jesus' response to Peter's question about how often to forgive, where "seventy-seven times" or "seven times seventy" comes with no mention of repentance at all!

Making repentance a prerequisite to forgiveness satisfies our innate sense of justice. If as Christians we cannot retaliate or satisfy our thirst for vengeance, at least we can require repentance. The reason heartfelt apology works effectively to set the stage for reconciliation is that it expresses contrition and repentance. It can go a long way toward restoring the moral harmony that has been damaged by an offense. Adding some kind of restitution to visible signals of shame and audible words of repentance is likely to soften our hearts further toward reconciliation. Repentance and restitution show that we are holding one another accountable for our actions and that there are tangible and painful consequences for breaking the laws that govern our life together. Both common sense and stable social order support this understanding.

The only problem with our conventional ideas about justice is the larger witness of Jesus' life and death.

Luke 17:3–4 notwithstanding, Jesus on the whole does not seem to make repentance a prerequisite for God's forgiveness. In healing the paralytic (Mark 2:1–12), he directly connects the man's healing to forgiveness of sins. Yet it is given not in response to any apparent contrition or repentance on the part of the paralytic but in response to the faith of those who brought him. Jesus calls Levi, identified as a sinner (tax collector), to become one of his disciples without requiring him first to confess or repent (Mark 2:14; Luke 5:27–28). While forgiveness is not explicit in the call to disciple ship, divine grace is clearly extended. In one of the most intriguing stories in the Gospels, Jesus essentially tells us how he himself understands the relationship between forgiveness and repentance. This story, told in Luke 7:36–50, deserves a closer look.

Jesus is eating dinner at the home of a Pharisee when a woman who is known about town as "a sinner" (for women this generally was a euphemism for prostitute) enters the house with an alabaster jar of ointment. She stands behind Jesus weeping, her tears bathing his feet, which she wipes dry with her hair; she kisses his feet and anoints them with ointment. The disgusted host, Simon, questions in his heart how Jesus could be a prophet if he doesn't even recognize what sort of woman this is. Jesus, reading his heart, tells a little story about two debtors and a generous creditor who cancels both debts. The story bears some parallels to the parable of the Unforgiving Servant in Matthew 18:23–35, but in this case, the difference between the debts is only tenfold. The point Jesus elicits from Simon is that the one forgiven the greater debt (five hundred denarii) will love the generous creditor more than the one whose canceled debt was only fifty denarii. Jesus then asks Simon to look at this woman, to see her for who she is. He points out that she has been engaged in acts of hospitality and signs of repentance since she entered. The key to the story lies in this statement: "Therefore, I tell you, her sins, which were many, have been forgiven; hence she has shown great love" (Luke 7:47).

I agree with Gregory Jones's interpretation of this passage in his theologically rich book *Embodying Forgiveness.*[1] It is not because the woman has shown repentance with tears that Jesus forgives her sins; rather, she shows repentance with tears because she has already known forgiveness and thus has great love for Jesus. It is her faith in his gift of pardon that saves her (v. 50).

Finally, we have the witness of the cross itself. In Luke's Gospel, Jesus' forgiveness of those who torture and kill him unjustly clearly takes place before any of his accusers or executioners give evidence of repentance. Indeed, the reason he gives for asking his heavenly Father to forgive them is that they don't understand what they are doing. They do not know to seek forgiveness because they don't fully understand themselves and certainly don't understand Jesus. Christ's words of forgiveness, from the place of his greatest physical agony and spiritual anguish, are the basis of a Christian understanding of God's unconditional love. The theme is picked up in Paul's letter to the Romans: "Indeed, rarely will anyone die for a righteous person. . . . But God proves [God's] love for us in that while we still were sinners Christ died for us" (5:7–8). It is the unbelievable generosity of divine love shown in Jesus' sacrifice that reveals to us God's love without prior conditions. Such love by its very nature calls forth from us a response of gratitude, repentance, and love. As Paul puts it earlier in the epistle, "Do you despise the riches of [God's] kindness and forbearance and patience? Do you not realize that God's kindness is meant to lead you to repentance?" (2:4).

From these central texts we see that repentance is indeed necessary to forgiveness, but not in the order we had assumed. It is not that unless we repent, God will refuse to forgive; it is, rather, that as we absorb the magnitude of God's undeserved gift of forgiveness, we can respond only with heartfelt repentance and gratitude. God's appeal to our defensive, fearful egos is the appeal of love. As L. William Countryman explains, "This is how the gospel, the good news, eventually delivers us from an unforgiving spirit. It doesn't work by admonishing us. . . . It works by overwhelming us with love."[2] Love aims to restore us to a new kind of life.

Is this not what we find in the parable of the Prodigal Son? God is represented in the figure of the father, who throws dignity to the wind and rushes out to meet his returning son. Filled with compassion, he embraces and kisses his son before the son's repentance speech begins and then calls for a robe and ring as symbols of full restoration of his son's place of dignity in the family. The only fitting response of the son to this generous welcome will be a life of humble gratitude, loving service, and willingness to forgive others their foolish and destructive choices. Thus, the father's response offers his son a new beginning within the family.

Do you hear echoes of the story of the Dakota

Sioux tribe from the first chapter? The Sioux murderer was not asked to repent as a condition of the tribe's acceptance. By their costly and generous act of embracing this man as their own kin, he will surely—out of a mix of pure shame and deep gratitude—repent and live a very different kind of life among them. The tribe's response offers this man a new beginning within the larger community. Surely it is the power of moral and spiritual persuasion that transforms and renews human life as God intends it to be.

RETHINKING THE NATURE OF JUSTICE

When we reverse the conventional relationship between repentance and forgiveness—from repentance yielding forgiveness to forgiveness yielding repentance—what happens to our understanding of justice? It may seem that justice as we have traditionally understood it has no place in this new arrangement. Yet there are two basic understandings of justice to consider as we grapple with this important question: retributive justice and restorative justice.

Retributive justice is by far the better known and is the norm in societies shaped by Western civilization. Our legal systems depend on an understanding of justice as punishment for the offender. The way to balance the scales of justice according to this norm is to impose penalties against the guilty—punishments from community service to prison to execution. We sometimes call this the penal system, reflecting our assumption that penalties are the proper way to achieve justice and give the victims satisfaction. Our sense of fairness tends to be satisfied to a certain extent by this form of justice. People should have to pay for their transgressions, and this involves suffering a loss of freedom if not one's life.

Restorative justice is more often the norm among the world's tribal peoples. The value of community and the desire to restore an offender to a sense of kinship with that person's community results in a very different approach to justice. For example, in New Zealand among the Maori, four elements inform their approach to modern-day teenage crime: (1) The form of accountability required for these young people is to be found by consensus involving the whole community; (2) the desired outcome is reconciliation rather than isolation and punishment of the offender; (3) the focus is less on blaming one individual than exploring the wider causes of wrongdoing; (4) concern for restoring harmony in the community is greater than concern for breach of the law.[3]

In general, indigenous societies see misbehavior as a distortion of communal harmony that calls for good teaching and healing. In some cases this might involve revealing publicly the offense within the offender's community. For the offender, this means the humiliation of facing daily those who know him or her best. However, the purpose is not to humiliate the person but to expose the negative behavior. The community affirms the worth and value of the offender and encourages that person to reform, but it shames the misbehavior. In other cases it might mean removing offenders from a stagnant, TV-centered environment and placing them in a certain kind of isolation (not incarceration) where they have no choice but to reflect inwardly. The purpose here is to teach individuals of their weakness alone and their dependence on the good of the whole community, in which they too have responsibility to uphold the peace. Mediation and community councils are the primary means of practicing such restorative justice.

What, finally, is the purpose of justice? Is punishment the goal, or restoration of a fully human life? God is far more interested in making new beginnings than in satisfying penal codes. God exercises judgment in the service of salvation and grants mercy in hopes of reclaiming us from the sad spectacle of our sin and its consequences. God has designs for a future radiant with renewal, harmony, and peace, and invites us to embrace the vision. The beauty of this vision is what the cross of Christ opens to all humanity if we will accept it. What about us? To forgive is to say yes to God's future, creating a path into that bright hope. By the grace of the Spirit, may we find freedom to do so gladly!

Study Guide

INTRODUCTION

THIS STUDY GUIDE IS ADAPTED FROM THE ORIGINAL LEADER'S guide titled "Learning Forgiveness: A Lenten Study," published by The Thoughtful Christian. The original guide provides instructions for a leader to facilitate a group of five to twenty persons.

This study guide may be adapted for groups of any size, including two people gathering for weekly study at a coffee shop. For each week there is an opening and closing prayer, an exploring activity, and a responding activity. The responding activity involves journaling in a notebook.

Most sessions do not require materials other than the book, Bibles, journals, and pens. The session for chapter 5 suggests a closing exercise that requires a bowl of water and stones.

BEGINNINGS

Luke 15:11–32

OPENING PRAYER

Great God, you are rich in mercy beyond our knowing. We thank you for the gift of your forgiveness of our sin, made known to us in Jesus. Help us to open our minds and hearts to your Holy Spirit in the days ahead as we travel together through this Lenten season. Show us what we need to understand, and help us learn how to practice forgiveness in all our relationships so that we might experience the renewal of common life you desire and offer to us in Christ our Lord, in whose name we pray. Amen.

EXPLORING

Read the parable in Luke 15:11–32, and then review and discuss the section in chapter 1 headed "Who Needs Forgiveness?" (pp. 2–5).

Have each person assume the role of one of the three characters in the parable. Ask each to imagine how, as that character, he or she would respond to the following questions:

- How do you see the other two persons in your family?
- What do you really want to say to each one?

⁂

With participants out of character, ask them to discuss some of the following questions:

- What insights arose from pretending to be one of the characters in the parable?
- What kind of healing does each brother need?
- Do you think the father needs to be forgiven? Why or why not?
- How are the various needs for forgiveness in this story connected?

RESPONDING

Lent is a season for spiritual practice. One of the most helpful practices for contemporary Christians is journaling, so the response in each session will be a brief time for doing just that.

Journal keeping has been used for centuries as a way to record insights, questions, prayers, feelings, and inner dialogues on matters of faith. It is a way of "meditating on paper" and of capturing movements in our relationship with God. Encourage participants to journal in whatever way is most comfortable. Complete sentences and grammar are less important than free and authentic self-expression.

Instruct participants to record insights and ongoing questions from this session in their journals and, specifically, to ponder how issues of forgiveness in their own lives are connected with the forgiveness of others in their webs of relationships.

CLOSING PRAYER

God of grace, thank you for the wonderful gift of human relationships. We acknowledge that often we take our deepest relationships for granted and find ourselves at odds with each other by putting our own interests first. Help us to see the larger picture of our hurts and hopes. By your generous mercy, give us humility and courage both to receive and to offer forgiveness so that our life together may be restored in the unity of love. We pray in Jesus' name and spirit. Amen.

Session 2

SELF-EXAMINATION

Psalms 51 and 139

OPENING PRAYER

Great God, shaper of every heart, you have searched us and you know us. You know who we are and what we are better than we do ourselves. In your great love, reveal us to ourselves. Help us to see what we need to see, help us to accept what you show us, and help us by your grace to act on self-knowledge so that we may become more like the One who courageously set his face toward Jerusalem to enter his passion so that we, too, might be freed for a fully human life. In his name we pray. Amen.

EXPLORING

Have each person choose whether to engage in examination of conscience or examination of consciousness, as described on pages 15–22 in chapter 2. Draw attention to the exercises below, and explain that each person should select one of the two exercises and spend the next fifteen minutes on it.

Practicing Self-Examination

Examination of Conscience: A Practice
in Penitence and Confession

1. Open your heart to God's grace, love, and light. Ask the Holy Spirit to help you see clearly what you need to see and are ready to see within yourself.
2. Respond to this question: Where do I find evidence in my life of a "heart turned in on itself"? You might find the questions on page 17 helpful in relating to your own forms of self-absorption.
3. Write a prayer of confession or your own psalm of penitence. Psalm 51 offers a general model.
4. Open your spirit to receive God's love for you. Accept inwardly a sense of divine forgiveness and invitation to a new future.

Examination of Consciousness: A Practice in Awareness

1. Acknowledge with gratitude that God knows

you through and through, loves you, and waits eagerly to summon out what you will become.

2. Ask the Holy Spirit to help you review with clarity the past twenty-four or forty-eight hours. Identify two or three instances in which God's grace becomes apparent to you as you reflect on the period under review. Were you aware of it at the time? How did you respond? If you recognized and responded in a way fitting the Christian life, give thanks! If you were unaware of divine presence or resistant to God's love, confess that and seek to become more aware and responsive in the future.

3. Write a psalm or prayer of praise, confession, and gratitude as it arises from your experience of self-examination.

Afterward, spend a few minutes discussing what people thought about the process, not the content, of their self-examination. Ask these questions:

– What was it like to reflect on your life in this way and to write your own psalm or prayer?
– What kind of "journey" did your feelings undertake in this process?

RESPONDING

Have participants journal about their experiences with self-examination by responding to the following:

- What have I learned in this process?
- Is self-examination a spiritual practice I want to continue in some way through Lent, and if so, how?
- In the spirit of self-examination, can I identify one thing I want to be forgiven for and one person I need to forgive? What first step can I take in each case?

CLOSING PRAYER

Ask people to review their psalms and prayers and to select one phrase, sentence, or stanza for speaking aloud as part of a group prayer of praise, confession, and gratitude. Indicate that this will be the corporate closing prayer today. The leader will begin. Explain that it is OK not to speak and that silent prayer is always appropriate. Conclude by praying the Lord's Prayer together.

HONESTY

Matthew 5:43–48 and 7:1–6

OPENING PRAYER

God of light, you shine in every part of creation and into every dark corner of our lives. Shed your light and grace today on our experience of enmity with others and enmity within our own divided selves. Help us to discover the motives behind our judgments and to begin seeing more clearly what it means to love our enemies. We pray in the name of him who loved us fiercely and tenderly while we were still your enemies. Amen.

EXPLORING

Read Matthew 7:3–5 and then the story of Abba Moses on page 29 in chapter 3. Discuss connections between these readings. Consider how we discover the sins we are blind to, either because we cannot or will not see them. Possible responses include self-examination; other forms of listening prayer such as *lectio divina* (a way of listening for the personal message of Scripture); discernment practices; listening to what others sometimes tell us about ourselves; directly asking those who know us best to help us see our weaknesses; and maturing through experience.

One of the best ways to discover aspects of ourselves we are blind to is to look closely at our enemies. It is often said that the things we can't stand in others reveal sides of ourselves we can't bear. What we dislike and reject most in ourselves we project onto those in whom we see those traits most clearly. They become bearers of our hidden faults, and we don't have to take responsibility for them. This dynamic is forceful individually and also corporately, such as between ethnic groups, religious groups, and nations.

Invite the group to a time of personal reflection with these instructions:

- Take a few minutes to identify several external enemies in your life: people in your family, church, work setting, or the government, whom you deeply dislike, criticize, judge, despise, feel angry with, or wish did not exist. Name them, and list as specifically as you can which of their traits make you feel so critical. Take another few minutes to identify several internal enemies in your life: attitudes, behaviors, reactions, feelings, perceived weaknesses or limitations that you deeply dislike, criticize, judge, despise, feel angry about, or wish did not exist. List the things about these parts of yourself you find so difficult to accept or acknowledge.

– Look at your two lists together. What do you notice? Are there any surprises or fresh connections for you? What can you learn from your external and internal enemies?

RESPONDING

Have participants journal about insights they have gained, things they have learned, or questions that have arisen for them from this exploration of inner and outer enmity.

CLOSING PRAYER

Lead the group in a time of intercessory prayer for an enemy. This form of prayer is called imaging intercession, and it engages the visual imagination. Those who can't visualize easily can use their "intellectual imagination" to get a sense of the person they are praying for. Invite participants to relax, take several deep breaths, and close their eyes. Read the following prayer at a relaxed pace, allowing ten to twenty seconds of silence where you see ellipses (. . .):

Come into God's presence, visualizing it as light, feeling it as love. . . . Remember that when we are in the divine presence we are never alone but are there together with all God's beloved children. Choose one of those children now, one you have real difficulty loving, who feels like an enemy. Allow yourself to see this person held in God's light and love, alongside yourself. . . . Imagine the things you find most difficult about this person as dark places, or hard shapes, or cold or hot spots in the mind, heart, or body. . . . Imagine how God's love affects these places inside the person. Visualize warmth and light surrounding, penetrating, and healing what needs to be healed. . . . Imagine the same light of God's love embracing and irradiating the dark or hard or cold or hot places in your own mind and heart. . . . Allow yourself to absorb this healing grace as fully as you can. . . . Finally, look at yourself and the other person again, side by side, and see if the picture looks or feels different. . . . Give thanks for whatever you have experienced in this time of prayer, and ask that the healing of wounds and changing of perspectives may continue. . . . Amen.

Session 4

REPENTANCE

Luke 23:32–43

OPENING PRAYER

O God, your love truly will not let us go. Help us to seek, and receive with gratitude, your costly forgiveness in Christ. Then, humbled and strengthened by your love, help us to seek forgiveness from those whom we have wounded or offended, knowing that our sins against one another are first of all sins against you, the author and giver and lover of life. We pray in the name of our Savior, Jesus Christ, whose suffering love redeems and transforms us. Amen.

EXPLORING

Discuss how we seek forgiveness from others, beginning with the matter of apology. Ask participants about
anything that struck them in reading about apology in
chapter 4. What did they learn, question, or feel con-
firmed in?

Read the following examples of apologies. After each
one, discuss whether or not it is a good apology, and
why.

1. "Honey, I'm really sorry that I exploded at you
   last night about not helping with dinner cleanup
   and getting the trash out. I know you were
   exhausted after the crazy week you've had at
   work, and you deserved some down time. I guess
   I was pretty tired myself from the baby being sick
   and from my friend Jodi being so rotten to me on
   the phone about what I had said to her kid. I'd
   had a really hard day, too."

2. "I want to say to you that I am deeply ashamed
   by what I have done in breaking our marriage
   vow. I am sorrier than I can say for the hurt I
   have caused you by my infidelity. I've been
   really foolish and selfish. I wish I could go back
   and erase what I did. All I can say is that I will
   try to make it up to you in any way I can, in any
   way you will let me. I'm prepared to go to coun-
   seling and do it seriously. I want to make a new

start, if you are willing. Please forgive me; with all my heart I ask you to please give me a second chance with you."

3. "Hey look, I'm sorry if what I said hurt your feelings. I didn't mean to, you know. I'm not really prejudiced about your ethnic background; I'm just a pretty rough-and-tumble kind of guy. And you're sort of a sensitive kind of gal."

❧

Write a letter of apology to someone living or dead from whom you feel the need for forgiveness. Decide whether or not to send your letter. If the intended recipient is not alive, then the act of writing itself is sufficient and may lead to further prayer.

RESPONDING

For journaling time, ask participants to follow one of the following instructions:

- Finish your letter if you haven't already.
- Journal on insights about yourself in relation to apology.
- Express your intentions about seeking forgiveness from others.

CLOSING PRAYER

Sing as a prayer several verses of "Dear Lord and Father of Mankind," a hymn that can be found in most traditional hymnals. Pay attention to the words of this familiar hymn while singing it as the prayer that it is.

Session 5

FORGIVING

Matthew 18:23–35

OPENING PRAYER

Holy God, your willing grace astonishes us when we consider what we, as human beings, have done to each other, to your creatures, and to this beautiful earth. Each of us has the seeds of destructiveness within us, yet we struggle with hard feelings when it comes our turn to forgive others. Soften the soil of our hearts with the spring rain of your grace; prepare us to be merciful as you are merciful. We ask this in the name of Christ, your mercy poured out upon us. Amen.

EXPLORING

Have participants brainstorm the best reasons they can think of to forgive others. Make a list. Responses may include these:

- God forgives us/Jesus set that example.
- I can see my own weaknesses or "shadow side" in the enemy.
- I have discovered the humanity of the offender.
- Holding onto a grudge or wanting revenge is ruining my life.
- I don't want to be the kind of person who can't forgive.
- Life is too short for hanging on to resentment.
- I want the pain passed on from earlier generations to stop with mine.
- The peace I want in this world begins with me.

Review the section of chapter 5 titled "Stories of Forgiveness" (pp. 51–55). Discuss which story especially drew people in or made them wonder what more was involved. Ask participants the following questions:

- How would you have reacted if you had been Kelly, Chris, or Ron in these situations?
- What thoughts or emotions would you find most difficult to get past?
- What do you think made it possible for these people to forgive?

⊗

Ask people to recall their answer to the weekly journaling question at the end of session 2: "Can I identify . . . one person I need to forgive?" (p. 77). If they have already forgiven that person, invite them to identify another, living or dead. Sometimes the person we most need to forgive is beyond the reach of this world but not beyond the reach of the Spirit. Allow a few moments for participants to identify someone. Tell everyone they now have an opportunity to work on offering forgiveness rather than receiving it.

Instruct participants to spend five minutes imagining how they might forgive the person they have identified. Ask questions like these to stimulate their imagination:

- How would you like to approach or encounter this person?
- What basic ideas or feelings would you want to express in conveying your forgiveness?
- What might it feel like afterward?

RESPONDING

Have participants journal on one or more of these topics:

- the way you imagined offering forgiveness;
- the feelings you may still be struggling with;
- your intentions about forgiving;
- what you are learning about yourself.

CLOSING

Engage in a simple ritual expressing where participants are in the process of forgiving. Use a bowl of water to represent forgiveness and new life, like the waters of baptism. Use stones to represent people identified since session 2 as those whom participants need to forgive.

Sit prayerfully and begin to hum "Amazing Grace." As people are ready, invite them to select a stone for each person they have forgiven over these past several weeks. Have them slip a stone into the water as a sign of letting go of the weight of resentment or bitterness. For each person they are not yet ready to forgive, they can simply place a stone on the table near the bowl.

Afterward, assure the group that there is no shame in not yet being ready to forgive. The stones around the bowl remind us all that we are still works in progress by God's grace. Bring the bowl back for the final session in case any are ready to let go of another stone.

BEGINNING AGAIN

Luke 7:36–47

OPENING PRAYER

Great God, your ways are truly not our ways, and your thoughts are infinitely higher than our thoughts. Help us to grasp the nature of your justice within the wider realm of your mercy, just as your ocean of love washes over the ocean of our sin. Reveal to us what we need to see within our own minds and hearts, and lead us in your ways of life-renewing truth and peace. In Jesus' name we pray. Amen.

EXPLORING

Direct attention to how this final chapter begins with a section on the relationship between forgiveness and reconciliation. It suggests that reconciliation can occur without direct forgiveness but that a certain interior release of the past must be in place for reconciliation to be authentic. The chapter speaks of "implied forgiveness" and offers a few stories to illustrate. Ask participants if they can think of stories from their own experience with family, friends, or colleagues that illustrate reconciliation without direct forgiveness. Invite the brief sharing of a story. Ask the storyteller if she or he thinks the situation involved a truly forgiving heart or just "sweeping things under the rug," and discuss how we might know the difference.

Point the group to this statement in the chapter: "The only problem with our conventional ideas about justice is the larger witness of Jesus' life and death" (p. 60). The next several paragraphs point to stories in the Gospels that seem to argue that repentance is not a prerequisite to forgiveness for God.

Read another beloved Gospel story, not addressed in the chapter, that may also be read in this light: John 8:1–11, the account of the woman caught in adultery. Discuss where repentance and forgiveness are found in this story. What is Jesus' expression of forgiveness here? Where is the element of repentance? Notice that Jesus' refusal to condemn this woman is an implicit expression of forgiveness and that his exhortation to her, "Go your way, and from now on do not sin again," is an implicit expectation of her subsequent repentance.

Discuss any connection people see between the woman caught in adultery and the murderer of the Dakota Sioux man from the story recounted on pages 7–10 in chapter 1. What "justice" does each sinner face? How is release from the death sentence likely to affect them? Discuss the distinction between retributive justice and restorative justice in the chapter.

Look at the two paragraphs in "Rethinking the Nature of Justice" in chapter 6 describing each approach (pp. 64–65). What is most convincing or promising about the idea of restorative justice? What anxieties do people have about its limitations?

RESPONDING

Have participants journal about one question below, and ask them to work on the other questions during the week.

- What relationship do I see between the emotions I most struggle with around forgiveness and my ideas of what serves justice?
- How do I respond inwardly to retributive justice? To restorative justice? Where do I stand on the relative value of each, and how would I justify my stance biblically and theologically?
- How does restorative justice connect with the idea that forgiveness involves us in larger issues of human community (from chapter 1)?

CLOSING ACTIVITY

Sing the first verse of "Joyful, Joyful, We Adore Thee" as an expression of gratitude and praise for God's great mercy and grace. If your hymnal includes the verse "Thou art giving and forgiving, . . ." sing this as well.

Remind the group that the water bowl signifying God's grace and the stones symbolizing persons yet unforgiven in our lives is near the door. If any are ready to slip another stone into the water, they are free to express their act of forgiveness before leaving. End the class by sharing signs of Christ's peace with each other.

NOTES

Chapter 1: Beginnings

1. Ella Cara Deloria, *Waterlily* (Lincoln: University of Nebraska Press, 1988), 192.

2. Ibid., 193.

3. Douglas Steere, *Dimensions of Prayer* (Nashville: Upper Room Books, 1997), 69.

Chapter 2: Self-Examination

1. This insight, along with other perspectives expressed here, are also treated in chapter 6 of my book *Soul Feast: An Invitation to the Christian Spiritual Life* (Louisville, KY: Westminster John Knox Press, 2005).

2. Richard J. Hauser, SJ, *Moving in the Spirit: Becoming a Contemplative in Action* (New York: Paulist Press, 1986), 55.

Chapter 3: Honesty

1. Ross Phares, *Bible in Pocket, Gun in Hand* (Lincoln: University of Nebraska Press, 1964), 136.
2. E. Glenn Hinson, "On Coping with Your Anger," *Weavings* 9, no. 2 (1994): 36–37.
3. *The Desert Christian: Sayings of the Desert Fathers,* trans. Benedicta Ward (New York: Macmillan, 1975), 138–39.
4. Ibid., 80.

Chapter 4: Repentance

1. Blaise Pascal, *Pensées,* ed. A. J. Krailsheimer, Penguin Classics (New York: Penguin Books USA, 1995), 289.
2. Carl D. Schneider, "What It Means to Be Sorry: The Power of Apology in Mediation," *Mediation Quarterly* 17, no. 3 (Spring 2000): 2.
3. Aaron Lazare, "Go Ahead, Say You're Sorry," *Psychology Today,* January/February 1995, 42, cited in Schneider, "What It Means to Be Sorry," 3.

Chapter 5: Forgiving

1. Thomas Merton, *The Wisdom of the Desert* (New York: New Directions, 1960), 75–76.
2. The stories of Kelly, Chris, Ron, and Karla are found in Johann Christoph Arnold's powerful book of such stories, *Why Forgive?* (Farmington, PA: Plough Publishing House, 2000).
3. The dialogue between Gary and Wayne is described by Carl D. Schneider in "What It Means to Be Sorry: The Power of Apology in Mediation," *Mediation Quarterly* 17, no. 3 (Spring 2000): 6–7.

Chapter 6: Beginning Again

1. L. Gregory Jones, *Embodying Forgiveness: A Theological Analysis* (Grand Rapids: Wm. B. Eerdmans Publishing Co., 1995), 160–62.